Ethereum

Discover The Ultimate Investment Plan

Contents

What Is Ethereum?

Smart Contracts
What Is Ether?
Ethereum Company
The Financial History Of Ether
Ethereum Programs

Difference between Ethereum and Bitcoin

How to Invest using Ethereum

How to Buy, Sell, And Store Ether
What Is Ethereum Mining?
How Ethereum will change the economy
How to enter the word of Cryptocurrency

Additional information you need to know if you want to purchase Ether

The Future Of Ethereum

What Is Ethereum?

There is a new way to invest and make money. When it comes to investing money, there is a new form taking over that is proving to be very successful. Ethereum is the new way people can invest their money. This form of cryptocurrency is used in Bitcoin and the future is looking promising.

 In the past couple of months, the price of Ethereum has greatly increased. This currency is still pretty new to most people and it will take some time and research to figure out how it works and the best plan for investing.

According to the definition from the Ethereum website, this is a new platform for application to run as they are programmed. They will run in that exact manner and there is not a chance of fraud happening. There is no censorship and no third parties will be involved in the manner in which this company runs and operates.

At first glance a person may not see anything special about Ethereum. When they run a program, they expect it to run as it is stated. There are some additional features that will set this program apart from others and ensure it cannot be tampered with. The code that is used for Ethereum has blockchains. This ensures it cannot be altered in any way. This also protects the program from being hacked or from the program being tampered with. This makes it safer to use.

A lot of time and research went into the development of the program, so it could be tamper proof. Good hackers can get into many programs, even safe programs, so the development for this took a lot of time and a great deal of effort. This tamper proof program, as well as the tamper proof technology, is ensured by cryptography. This uses the newest blockchain technology to ensure the program is safe to use. It is some of the most secure technology ever made.

In addition to having this blockchain technology as protection, this program is also decentralized on the blockchain software program. This will allow it to be joined with the cryptocurrency asset. This currency will also run on the Ethereum network, which will allow this to be safe and secure as well. A person will know that this program is going to protect their investment and they will not have to worry about losing everything due to hackers or computer malfunctions.

• Smart Contracts

Using the Ethereum technology a person will be able to build and carry out smart contracts. They will also be able to perform operations in Distributed Autonomous Applications which is a program that is also known as DApps. A person can perform a number of operations and be free from censorship. There is also no downtime or wait time between transactions. Users find that the best part of using this program is that no third party will have access to any of the information or any part of the process. This will save them from hacking and will also block any unwanted information. Many people feel that this offers additional protection as well.

This program also has its own language. It uses the language known as Solidity. This has been used to write the contracts, as well as the DAapps. The cryptocurrency asset that is also known by the name Ether is used to help with the writing of the apps, as well as the different contracts. This is why Ethereum has become known to many as what is considered as programmable money.

This program was first developed back in 2013. Vatalik Buterin, who is a Russian programmer, began to work on this program. He tested and retested. He was not satisfied with his program until he perfected it. Ethereum was announced to the world in January 2014. It was at the North American Bitcoin Conference located in the city of Miami in the United States where this program was first introduced to the masses.

People were amazed at his program and it was able to do things that the Bitcoin program could not do. This program was focusing on coding and was looking to handle all aspects of smart contracts. Everything could be done by the program and there was no human needed to keep it running.

Dr. Gavin Wood joined the development of this program in July of the same year the Ethereum Foundation began. This foundation further developed the software and in no time, it was a major contender. It was able to raise $18 million dollars before even being released. This money was just in the presale of the Ether tokens.

In addition to the founders, there are some others who have helped with the development of this program. Jeffery Wilcke is in charge of setting up the Go programming language on Ethereum and making sure everything is being read and understood correctly. Ming Chan is the executive director of the company. She is in charge of the legal matters as well as making sure that this program is following all the regulations.

There is still some confusion as to how this program will be produced. Many want to know when it will be available to the masses and when they will be able to use it. Ethereum is not going to be produced in masses and it is not going to be minced. It is the Ether program that people will be using.

What Is Ether?

Ethereum is a network that uses blockchain technology. This is the coding and the program that cannot be hacked. This is the program that is safe and secure. Ether is the cryptocurrency that is going to be used. Ether is the technology that will be used to keep the program running and will be what is used when users go onto the platform of this technology.

Ether is also sometimes referred to as ETH. This is going to be issued to the users. It will be issued as an annual linear rate. This rate will be determined with the block mining process. The rate will be 0.3 times the annual amount that the ETH has raised. This amount will be the presale rate.

During the presale a great deal of Ether was sold. In fact, 60,102,216 units were sold before the platform was even officially released. This is very impressive for a wholesale total. When this amount is multiplied by the rate of 0.3 it generates just over 18 million dollars per year. This is an impressive amount, especially since it is still very young.

When purchasing Ether, a person can relax knowing that their money is safe and secure. The Ether is backed by the Ethereum program which cannot be hacked or modified. This is one of the reasons why this program has become so appealing and people are willing to put their money on this platform.

Ether also works quickly. Around every 12 seconds a new Ethereum block can be mined. When this happens, there is a reward for the mining. The computer that has successfully mined this Ether will receive a reward. The reward for this mining is 5 Ether. With the rate that this is mined the amount can be built up very quickly.

• Ethereum Company

There are different ways to mine the Ether so that a person can receive the reward they are looking for. They can mine the Ether using the CPU mining or GPU mining. The mining blocks are found on the Ethereum blockchain and they are also protected by the anti-fraud measures that this program is built upon.

This company is based off of Market Capitalization rates. These rates are also known as the Market Cap. Currently, this company is valued at $10 billion in market cap. This is around a third of the market cap that Bitcoin currently has. While this amount may not seem like a lot, it is still worth investing in. The company is still new, and people need to get used to it being on the market. They also need to get familiar with the new technology that is being used.

On this market the value of one unit of Ether is $126. This amount has seen a drastic increase since it was released. In not even a year the value has increased by ten times its amount. From February 2017 to the end of 2017 the value increased by a great deal. Many are still waiting to see if this value will continue to grow and how much more it will increase.

There are some common wallets that the Ethereum is compatible with. This program is able to work with Hardware Wallets that include the likes of Trezor and Ledger Nano S. It works with popular forms on mobile wallets that are used around the world. These wallets are compatible with different operating systems. Jaxx and Coinbase can be used by people with the Android or the Apple IOS operating system.

Ethereum Wallet is only currently available for people that have the IOS operating system. Those that are using a desktop device can have several different types of wallets as well. Coinbase is popular on these devices. That, along with Windows, Mac, or the Linux operating systems can use Jaxx as well. There are web wallets that can be used such as Coinpayments. If a person prefers to use a paper wallet they can choose from MyEtherWallet, Classic Ether Wallet, or EthAddress to use their money.

• The Financial History Of Ether

The blockchain is what draws many people to this new online platform. The Decentralized Autonomous Organization (DAO) was developed on the blockchain that is used by Ethereum. This made the company the first Venture Capital Firm that was not owned and was not operated by any one individual. This firm uses a smart contract to work with the DAO tokens. When this program hit the crowdfunding back in June of 2016 it was able to reach $150 million in no time at all.

The problem with the DAO was that it was hacked. There is where the Ethereum program is different. This program has additional security measures so that it cannot be hacked. Due to this hacking incident Ethereum decided that additional security measured needed to be taken. They developed the Hard Fork which makes any form of hacking programs and techniques that hackers are using invalid. This lead to the formation of the blockchain. The classic blockchain became known as the ETC or the Ethereum Classic.

The Ethereum Classic blockchain worked well, but they were not satisfied. They continued to work until the Block 18200 was developed where the Hard Fork was used. Users that were not able to support this Hard Fork used an older version of the program. They got the protection of the blockchain, but they were not able to get all of the upgrades that the other version could get.

Both versions of the blockchain can use ETC as part of the trade platform, as well as part of the exchange platform. They will get the same functions that the decentralized apps have, as well as the smart contracts.

There is a version of this program that is available for every user to help keep their information safe and well protected. The name of this program is Golem. This program is the first of its kind that is decentralized and uses an open sourced supercomputer. This was developed just for the Ethereum program and can be used by any user of this program.

There is an interesting way that this computer gets it information. The computational power comes directly from the combination of smaller personal laptops, as well as giant data centers. This allows it to contain a great deal of information and get this information safely to the users at a fast pace. Users get to enjoy some great features. They can use this program to run their website, they can use it to calculate many different types of complicated computational issues and problem, and they can even run it to run long codes. If a person needs additional computational resources, they can use this for that purpose as well. This program is even able to use miners and mine cryptocurrencies.

This program also opens up a number of economic opportunities. This computing power can be used, and a person can actually use it to make money. This program allows them to rent space on their personal computer to other users. Brass Golem is another program presented by the Golem program and is the first application that can help the computer run much quicker.

It can even help the graphics load faster and can help make mining quicker so that a person can make even more money. This is just one of the programs that is based off of the Ethereum blockchains. There are a number of other programs that are based off of these blockchains and are used for the purpose of making money as well as security.

Stock it uses the Ethereum blockchains and combines with it the IotS system that will allow the users to have even more features and additional security access. This network will allow people all around the world to sell their goods and do so in a secure manner thanks to the blockchains. Around sixty –six percent of the world is willing to share their goods and sell their assets if they are able to make a profit off of it.

This program will allow people to connect and is an active trade marketplace. This makes all things, including space on the computer and physical items available for rent. A person can search by their location or by the item they are looking to rent out to others for a price. This platform allows a person to rent out their apartment or home, vehicle, office space, and just about anything else when they are not using it. This can also be thanks to the smart technology that has been programmed onto the Ethereum blockchains.

Ethereum Programs

The Airbnb program is another program that was developed by Ethereum and another reason why this company is gaining in popularity. They use smart objects that are completely controlled by the computer and other smart locks. These items are programmed and developed on the Ethereum program. A person can the operate them on their smartphone or computer. They are simple to use, and they are secure.

Support is being developed for the average users. The Ethereum program is using blockchains to help with this program as well. This system is easy to use and wants to help develop a global system for people to get their goods. They want to work with individuals, businesses, bots, and devices that will allow users to work with a simple program. They will allow a user to have access to drones controlled by DHL or even FedEx and they are going to be operated by the Ethereum smart contract. This will allow a person to get their package within a given time frame.

This program will also require a user to verify their identity. This can help ensure that packages are not stolen and will make it to the person who ordered it. No package will be left at the door and a person will no longer have to make a trip to the post office or the FedEx store if they were not home at the time of delivery. While this service is still under development and the blockchains are still being worked on, people who have heard about this program are very excited about it and cannot wait until it is finished. This app would make things much easier for the average person who shops online and businesses that need to receive and ship their goods.

Ethereum is also using their smart contracts and blockchains for entertainment purposes. They are working on SngularDTV. This is the first television set in the world that will be decentralized. A person will be able to watch television and it will run on a royalty management platform which will help the companies decrease the chance of fraud and will make sure their copyright laws are protected.

This system will help control both management rights and entertainment rights. They will make sure any funds and profits are shared between the creators, writers, investors, actors in the series, as well as the crew members. This will help keep any fraud from interfering with the shows as well. There is no centralized party and the funds for the show cannot be taken away. The funds will get to the designated parties by the use of codes and smart contracts. There are no third parties involved, which takes away the threat of fraud. This entire payment system is run by the Ethereum blockchains, as well as the crypto tokens that are used on this system.

This company is also looking to get into blogging as well. They understand the popularity of blogging and the need to keep this information secure. While some people blog for fun there are people that use their blog to make money. They want to make sure their money is not stolen and the blockchains can make sure everything is secure.

EtherTweet is the blog program that is using this new technology. The Ethereum blockchains control the entire microblogging services that are offered. In addition to regular blogs microblogging is similar to a site such as Twitter. In each post up to 160 characters are used. The difference with this program is that the characters are decentralized before they are posted thanks to the Ethereum blockchains.

This will allow a user to create their content, share it, and take it down if they want to. There is no censorship about what they can and what they cannot post. This program runs off blockchains alone and there is no third party. If the content that is published becomes popular and is upvoted the user that developed it can get paid with Ether.

Difference between Ethereum and Bitcoin

Ethereum and Bitcoin may both be online platforms and do have some similarities, but at the same time they are very different. Bitcoin has been around for a longer period of time. These programs have been in existence and open for use since 2008. Ethereum is a fairly new program compared to this. It has been online and used since 2015. Bitcoin was released by the Genesis Block Mined and Ethereum was making money thanks to presales.

Both of these use blockchains that are called Proof of Work. Ethereum is currently working on developing a POS system. While it is not completed yet, there are plans that are currently being tested and developed. Bitcoin uses digital currency to help a person send and receive money. Ethereum also uses a form of digital currency. They can have contracts with other programs as well. They use smart contracts to help other companies send and receive money as well over the internet.

The currency that is used on Bitcoins is also referred to as Bitcoins and sometimes they can be called Satoshi. Ether is the currency that is used by the program Ethereum. The algorithm that is used by Bitcoin is the SHA- 256. Ethash is the algorithm that is used by Ethereum.

Bitcoin has a bloc time of up to 10 minutes. This is standard. Many people think that Ethereum is so much quicker than this program. It is so quick that all transactions are done in less than a minute. It takes between 12 and 14 seconds for actions to be completed. The mining s used by Bitcoin is the ASIC miners, while Ethereum uses the GPS. Currently Bitcoin is not scalable, while Ethereum is. There are some major differences between these online programs even though they are both involved in the trading of currency.

That is not where the difference in the programs end. Bitcoin is an electric system that allows peer to peer transfer of money. This digital money stores and hands all past transactions which will allow for the easy transfer of this currency. Ethereum can do more than this program. Due to the blockchains they can also handle the transaction and the exchange of currency. They can handle different accounts and can even help with these accounts thanks to the programming logic.

For example, if a Person A is looking to send $100 to Person B Person A must have enough money in their account in order for this transfer to happen. If they do not have enough money in their account, the transaction will not take place. The logic on their program is able to check all transactions before they are performed to make sure they are accurate, and everything goes smoothly.

This program also uses several different types of codes. Once these codes are used for the transaction it will instantly be stored on the blockchains. There is no specific time that it is stored for. This information can be stored forever. This will help a person, or a business look at future transactions and this information can assist with the process of making decisions.

Ethereum is different than Bitcoin due to these additional features. While both programs allow for the transfer of currency, Ethereum takes it a step further. They will allow the use of smart contracts as well.

Ethereum also takes away the need for a third party to get involved in a transaction. The more bodies that the currency has to travel through the greater the chances that a mistake can be made, the money may be misplaced, and there is always the chance that fraud can occur. Third parties are often used to help complete the transaction. Ethereum is able to execute the transaction without the use of a third-party service. As technology matures and advances this program will continue to improve and save users both time and give them peace of mind.

There are many advantages of using the Ethereum platform. Many people are finding interest in this program due to decentralization and additional safety. This program can reduce errors and failure in transfers. Only one contact is used, making the entire process much safer. This will also increase the speed at which the transaction is completed. This will help save time. When a third party is used the price for the transaction is often higher. The third party needs to add money for their services. They need to get paid and make money for their part in the transaction. The use of Ethereum can help reduce costs since there is no third party that will need to be paid.

While Bitcoin and Ethereum are both in the currency business and help people transfer money, they want to be clear that they are not in competition. Both companies have stated that they are not competitors. They both coexist in the online world. They are used to help people solve problems and have features that some people prefer over the others. Both companies have stated that they are looking to help people solve problems that they have in the real world. They are also open to new opportunities and are both looking to expand the services that they offer in the future. Both operations are constantly looking for ways to improve the technology that they use and make things more efficient for their users.

How to Invest using Ethereum

For those looking to invest using Ethereum it is easy to get started. In order to get started a person should purchase Ether. They can make this purchase using a credit card, wire transfer, and they can even use cash. This is one of the most popular exchanges. It is important to make this purchase only from the real Ethereum site. There are other sites out there that are looking to sell Ether as well. Sites such as eToro will try to sell Ether, but they may not have the exact price. A person may be getting less currency for the money that they point out. Also, coins cannot be sent from site such as eToro to other users.

The only thing that they can do on sites like this is buy and sell with flat currency. This will not help a person make money, but will allow them to conduct some transactions. When purchasing directly from Ethereum a person will be able to do more with the Ether and they will know they are getting the actual exchange rates.

Ethereum can also be purchase using Coinbase. A person should check and make sure that Coinbase is available in their country. There are many countries that will work with this program, but there are some that still do not accept this. In order to get an account a person has to go to Coinbase and click on setup an account. They need to add a method for payment to their account. Payments that are accepted include credit cards or a person can use their bank account to directly transfer in funds.

A person will then go to the buy and sell option and they will enter the amount of Ethereum that they wish to purchase. Once they have determined the amount they want they will click on the buy button. Coinbase does charge a fee for the processing and sending of Ether to their users. The fee will vary from 1.4 percent to 3.9 percent. This percentage rate will be based on the method of payment that was used. If a person is paying using their credit card, they will often have to pay the higher interest rate on their transactions. Coinbase is a fairly easy program to use and can be used by those that are not the most familiar in purchasing and trading online currency.

How to Buy, Sell, And Store Ether

A person can also purchase Ether through the site Cex.io. This site sells Bitcoins as well. A credit card will need to be used for the purchase. The fees that this site charges are already included in their exchange rate. This can be a reason why the exchange fee is higher on this site than on other sites. The exchange rate for 1 Ether can be as much as 7 percent higher than other sites but a person will not be surprised with transaction fees when they go to complete their purchase.

When a person is looking to purchase Ether on this site they will need to open an account. A person will then add their credit card or bank account information as their payment method. They will than select the buy and sell feature. They will enter the amount of Ether they wish to purchase and will then click the buy button. It is that easy to complete the purchase. These are just a couple of the sites that can be used to purchase Ether and get started with online investing.

Once a person has purchased their Ether they will be able to see their purchase information on the blockchains. For some this information can be a little confusing to read. There is a complete online guide to learning how to read this transaction and understanding their purchase receipt.

There are many people that may have an interest in working with Ethereum, but they may not be ready to purchase Ether. Many people just want to use this site to make a profit and are looking to use Ether for investment purposes. There are several ways that they can do this as well. In order to do this a person can make a profit on their exchange rate. They can use CFS or contracts for differences to begin to make money. Instead of purchasing the actual Ether a person will trade them based on the different exchange rates.

This is often recommended for those that have some trading experience. A person is going to be risking their money like they do with other forms or trading. There are over 500 companies that are looking to trade Ether. A person needs to study the different exchange rates to make sure they are getting a good deal and they will be able to make a profit on their exchanges.

· What Is Ethereum Mining?

A person can also invest in the Ethereum world through mining. This is considered the old-fashioned method of investing. A regular person can use their computer to make money. They are going to be able to unlock tokens using the Ethereum platform. There are several ways to unlock these tokens. If a person is good at math they can solve complicated math problems, as well as problems of logic to earn these tokens.

This is part of the cryptographic system. This system can be rather complete and complicated and in order to work with it a person is going to need a computer that has a very powerful processer. They need to maintain the GPUs as well, which is not an easy thing to do. The downside to this is that the amount of the rewards will decrease over time. While mining can help a person make a profit and get started, they may not be able to make a lot of money using mining in the long run.

When a person is looking to purchase tokens for their use they need to keep in mind that there are different symbols that are being used. There is the ETH symbol, as well as the ETC symbol. ETH is the most up to date version of this program and is constantly updated. ETC is the classic version and this is rarely used any longer. When people talk about purchasing tokens they are more than likely talking about purchasing ETH.

Many investors like using Ethereum and trust their system. They are in the business of making money and so far, are doing well with this form of investment. Many people like that this system as it is as secure as it can get. They also like that all the regulations and all aspects of trading are transparent. There is nothing that is hidden and there are no secret charges that are tacked onto the end.

This program also makes it easy to trade with different currencies. An investor can use this program to trade between different nations and different countries. This will allow a person to look for the best return rate on their investment and make the most money when they buy and sell these items. Now that the word is out about Ether and this form of trading people are looking to get involved before it is too late. Since this company made a lot of money during the presale people want to be able to get in on this before there is nothing left.

Every investor has different expectations and are willing to take a different level of risk. While many people have made money with this program and by using Ether, there is still some risk involved. Whenever investing is involved there is always going to be a risk, and nothing is a sure thing. A person should invest in this if they are tolerant to risk. While sales have been good so far and people have made a lot of money a person needs to be willing to risk the changes in the currency, as well as the conversion rates.

In order to make money a person is going to need to be patient. The rates change all the time and a person will want to hold onto their Ether, so they can get the best return. This can take a long time. If a person wants to maximize their profit they should be willing to wait for two to three years. The money will be tied up for that time. Like all investments a person should not invest more money than they can afford to lose. If for some reason things do not work out as expected, a person should not put themselves into a dire financial situation.

Within 48 hours of investing the price of Ether dropped 40 percent. This can make some people very nervous. Some people may have been near a panic, but things did not stay like this. Within the next couple of days, the Ether was worth their highest value yet. While the initial drop was very scary the market was able to recover. as well as prosper. A person has to be able to be emotionally strong enough to handle the dips in the market and not panic right away.

How Ethereum will change the economy

·

There are many things that Ethereum is looking forward to developing in the future. While they are one of the safest platforms in the online world they are always looking for ways to expand the products and the services that they are offering to their users. They want to become more than a site that is just used for digital currency. They are also looking to increase their use of smart contracts. They would like to see more people, including major businesses use smart contracts in order to exchange currency.

This company is also looking to change the way that business is conducted. They are looking to change the way that economies are run and operated. They are looking to change things from a centralized economy to a decentralized way of doing business. They will help remove any borders and limitations. This will allow people and businesses all over the world to conduct business transactions with each other.

The decentralization of the economy will change the way many industries work and are operated. It will have a positive impact on the way that finance companies operate, the way the entertainment industry collects their earnings, and the way real estate transactions are completed. There will be a change in the academic world, healthcare, insurance, social media, and even those companies that operate in the public sector. Just about every industry will be impacted.

Looking at the development of the blockchains the future for Ethereum looks bright. Many people want to conduct transactions knowing that their information and the currency that they are using is safe from hackers and all transactions are secure. Since the DAO has been hacked people have been turning their attention to the blockchains from Ethereum. This company is the most traded platform for cryptocurrency in 2017. This company is on its way up as its popularity continues to increase.

When investing online a person is using cryptocurrency. This currency is a digital asset that will work in place of money for an exchange. It has the same designated value as money would only it is safer to work with online where cash cannot be exchanged hand to hand. This form of currency is used to ensure that transactions are safe and secure. It stands in the place of assets when a person is trading online.

These are considered to be a form of digital currency and have also been called virtual currency. Bitcoin was one of the first forms of decentralized cryptocurrency that has been used online. Since this time the world of digital currency has evolved and now a person can purchase Ether as a form of this currency. There are now over a thousand different forms of cryptocurrency that are used online.

Many are made to decrease the amount of currency in circulation, but the main form of this is to allow people to make exchanges and investments online. Modern technology is used to control the flow of this money. This currency is often encrypted so that it is safe to use and cannot be hacked or sold without the proper authorization. A person can also enjoy anonymity when they are using this money online. This form of payment is now being accepted all over the world. Virtual currencies are being accepted all around the world.

This form of currency is legal, but for some governments it is harder to keep track of as well as harder to regulate. Some countries have developed strict rules that need to be followed, while other countries have banned the use of cryptocurrency. They are making policies to ensure it is properly regulated and accounted for. China is one of the countries that have banned the use of using Bitcoins by banks and by other industries. They have not decided how they are going to keep track of this currency at this point, so they put a ban on it since 2014. In Russia online currency is legal but according to the law it is still illegal to purchase any form of goods with anything else besides the Russian ruble.

In the United States the IRS has decided that use of cryptocurrency including the Bitcoin, as well as Ether will be treated as property tax instead of currency. A person will still need to account for any profits that they make and pay a capital gains tax on this money. This form of currency is legal and can be used as long as a person is reporting it accurately and paying their share of taxes on it.

As this form of currency increases governments want to make sure a person can use it safely and will not have to worry about online criminals that are looking to steal their money or allow this currency to become a serious threat to society. Transactions are often done though banking systems that are independently owned and operated. Some governments are still able to keep track of this system, so on any income that a person may see, including income they make buying and selling Ether, they need to be prepared to pay taxes on it.

How to enter in the word of Cryptocurrency

When a person is looking to enter the world of cryptocurrency they need to make sure they are getting this currency from a trusted source and that this currency is accounted for. When the money is regulated for a new online system it needs to pass initial coin offerings. This program is used as a startup venture and there are a number of rules and regulations that the currency and the offering body need to meet in order for the currency to be used. There are additional regulations if it is going to be sold and used as a means of trading online. Ethereum had to go through a number of banks and bankers, as well as regulations so that it could be used as a legal tender.

While cryptocurrencies may operate outside of traditional government instructions there are still some rules to economic that is followed even when it is strictly traded over the Internet. As of December 2017, this form of currency is making a lot of people a lot of money and is high in value. Currently it is valued at over $600 billion in all forms. A daily high in the trading of cryptocurrency has reached over $50 billion dollars in a single day.

There are different ways that the use of this currency is measured. There is the Crypto Index CRIX which was developed by statisticians at the Humboldt University of Berlin, as well as those at the Singapore Management University. This information dates back to 2014 and has shown how the use of this currency has changed. It shows the rate at which this currency is being used, as well as the rate at which new forms of currency is being developed.

A person can track the history and the uses of several currencies, including Ether. They can check and see how frequently this currency is being traded, which will help them with their investments. They can also use this information to determine if it is a good time to buy or to sell in order to make the biggest profit. This is one of the first indexes of its kind that will be able to look at the cryptocurrency market and show how it has changed. This index is updated often so a person can use it to help them with decisions and know that they are getting the latest information.

There is another index that is used to help measure the transfer and the use of cryptocurrency. The CCI30 Crypto Currencies Index is another tool that can be used by people that are looking to make the most money on their investment. This index watches over 30 forms of crypto currencies that are used all over the world, including the Ether.

A team of professionals, including those that have advanced training in math, data analysis, traders, and economics manage this system. They use an index of 30 fixed numbers and each of the rates are based on a percentage that uses the square roof of the smothered market capital of the form of currency. This is rather complicated to figure out and this index is only updated quarterly during the year. It takes a lot of time to go through this formula and then use it with the weighed moving average, as well as the performance in the market.

Luckily when a person goes to read this report they can track their currency and see if the performance has increased or decreased from quarter to quarter. A person can also compare currencies to see how they are performing against each other. This index just started in January 2015. Since this time, it is free and available for the public to use. This index is used to help a person develop a sound investment plan and help them increase the chances of making a profit based on how they are going to invest in this new form of currency.

There is additional information that has been made available to people looking to find out more about cryptocurrencies and for those looking to make investments with this form of currency. There is a peer review academic journal that has been released named the Ledger. This journal contains information about cryptocurrencies, as well as the buying and the selling of the different currencies. A person can use this to find out more information about these currencies in general.

There is even some information about a specific currency in this academic information. A person can read up on the different types of related technology as well. The Ledger is published by professionals at the University of Pittsburgh. The information that is found in this journal is checked and then it is timestamped. Once the information has been timestamped it is used as part of the Bitcoin blockchain.

While there are a number of authors that are allowed to have their work published in this collection, they need to include their Bitcoin address on the first page of this report. This will help them see that the report is authentic and someone that has experience with this medium is publishing information.

Cryptocurrency can be obtained in several different ways. A person can use real currency to purchase this online currency. They should research the different exchange rates before making a purchase. Some sites may give more currency for the dollar than others. In addition to using real currency to pay for online currency, they can use mining to get cryptocurrency such as Ether. A person will need to use their computer to mine for it.

In order for this currency to be used there need to be merchants as well as online trading vendors that will accept it. If no one were to accept the currency, then it would have little use. A person also needs to work with companies that will protect their information as well as their currency. If for some reason this currency is attached by a virus or other malware it cannot be replaced. This can also happen with data loss. That is why Ether is protected with codes and systems that are not able to be hacked. This adds an additional level of security knowing that their money is well protected.

All of the transactions that are conducted using cryptocurrency are stored in a ledger that is open to the public for viewing. The identities of the person making the purchases are encrypted, but the other information can be used for analyses, and record keeping. This will help ensure that the transactions are valid. Coins are also being checked as part of a transaction block chain to help reduce the chance of fraud.

All transactions need to be confirmed and that is where mining comes into play. Once a transaction comes into play it becomes part of the public ledger. In order for the transaction to be part of this ledger it gives needs to be completed. In order for it completed a miner has to solve a very complex math puzzle. Anyone can have access to this puzzle and if they are able to solve it correctly, it can become part of the transactions. When these transactions are solved they become block, so are on the ledger.

Several of these transactions are able to build a blockchain and make a blockchain ledger. Once the block becomes part of the ledger as well as all corresponding information it is permanent and cannot be deleted or changed in any way. For miners who can solve these puzzles, they will get new coins added to their digital wallet. This can be compared to a form of payment for solving the problem. The mining process can also add value to these coins. This then becomes known as a proof of work system.

Additional information you need to know if you want to purchase Ether

There is other information that a person should know when they are looking to purchase Ether and work with the cryptocurrencies. Adaptive scaling will help ensure that these currencies can work on both small and large scales. If a person is trading, they need something that is going to be able to work on a large scale and handle a certain amount of traffic. Many of the cryptocurrencies use a proof of work system to help with the verification process. This makes the transactions hard to solve, but once they are it allows the person who solved them to be rewarded with new currency.

When using digital currencies, a person often uses a pseudonym. This will allow a person to keep their digital currency, including Ether in a digital wallet that is encrypted for their protection. A person will have control over their own digital wallet and it will have an address that is encrypted. This is not attached to their real identity. A pseudo name will be used to attach a person to the coins that they hold in a digital wallet. Since the ledger is open to the public this is done for security purposes. Now groups of others will not be able to get information about individuals and will not be able to find a specific person's digital wallet. This will help prevent theft as well.

With the increase in the use of digital currency many people are taking notice of Ethereum and they are thinking that they want to get in on the purchase of Ether. There are new milestones that are being added to this program and they are looking to make a bright future. Ethereum Homestead is currently in development. This will be a new blockchain and app platform there have been some hints about the features to the public. This program has around 1,1,50,000 blocks in the main network and is being updated by the Hard Fork.

The rewards for the block and for solving one of the mining problems is currently 5 Ether per block. Mining is still possible in this. There are some additional features as well and there is a protocol that needs to be followed. Computer networking is changing the way that they want to make blocks and they are leaving some things open in this program, so it can be upgraded in the future. Ethereum applications, including Go were updated for this version, making it look a little different than what most people are used to seeing.

Ethereum is currently working on the third phase of its new project. It is working on building the Metropolis which is said to be the future of this project, as well as the way that people transfer currency over the Internet. The Metropolis is considered to have complete interface, as well as applications for those that may not have a great deal of technical experience or a great deal of experience in online trading. This is considered to be the phase of this program being designed for the mainstream users.

The company wants to make sure that everyone can use Ethereum even if they do not know very much about computers or how online currency works. This form of the project will be more hands-on than users are used to on the current platform. The projects will be improved and optimized as well and there will be additional features.

These new features will include the way that money is processed and accessed.

There will be A Dapp Store featured as part of a Mist Wallet. This will help users understand how powerful this entire network is and will help them with their transactions. This is going to be considered the prime aspect of the company. With this new technology the prices for Ethereum, as well as Ether are expected to increase. Now is the time to buy if a person is looking to make their money in this manner. Once this become mainstream prices will increase as there will be a higher demand and more people looking to purchase Ether.

Serenity is also a new feature that is looking to be added to Ethereum. This part of the program will have a lot to do with the mining aspect. The developers are working to change the proof of work concept that the system currently uses. There will make a difference in the way that things work. The mining will not need Ethereum mining to operate since this will mess up the electricity that the computer power is turning into heat. The company is looking to take a green approach to the way that they operate.

Mining uses up a lot of power and in addition to reducing the amount of energy that is used, they need to change the way that they power up. Proof of work is going to be changed to proof of stake. In order to make this change and help out the users and the environment, it is going to take some time to formulate this program and get it working properly.

In addition to using less power this change is looking to make the network work faster and work in a more efficient manner. It will also help reduce energy costs of running the computer and taking the time to mine. Mining can be complicated, and it does take a lot of time to complete this task. All this time the computer is working in overdrive and using up a great deal of energy. Serenity is still in development and the details are still pending. They are being improved upon and the way to implement them is still being worked on as well.

If a person is looking to get in on the Ethereum site and make some money they should do so sooner than later. As of November 2017, the price for Ethereum was around $308. The year to date price change at this time was 3,700 percent. This organization is currently valued around $29 billion, which is very impressive. While Bitcoin is valued at $97 billion for being a new company, it is making a good start. To have a value in the billions of dollars is a rather impressive accomplishment even in the dot com world.

There is still plenty of coins that can be found in Ethereum and still plenty of coins that can be mined. There is no limit placed on the number of Ethereum tokens that are available and there is no limit to the amount that a person can build up. There are also some applications that people can use on their platform to further help them out in their financial quest. A person can design smart contracts and use this as a way to collect payment and a new way to receive payment.

There are also the initial coin offerings which can be a way to exchange currency online. According to researchers and economists, this site is one to be trusted and will be around for a longer period of time. Harry

Dent, who is an economist and has written several books on the subject, feels that Ethereum is going to make blockchains easier and is a more credible site than others. He also stated that Ethereum is looking to improve the entire industry and is more than just a major trend. It will change the way people exchange currency online.

Major companies have developed their own systems based on the Ethereum model. The major bank JP Morgan built their program Quorum based on the protocol of Ethereum. They used these techniques to make their network faster and safer for their customers. The customers are taking notice as well. Transactions are being processed at a faster pace and bill payments and even money transfers are being handled in a faster and a more efficient manner.

Other companies are using the blockchains that are offered by Ethereum as well. NotarEth, which is an online notary service, is using these blockchains to help with customer service. They can now verify a person's identity over the Internet using the blockchains to make sure everything is safe and secure. The customer will not have to provide their ID and will get a document stamped. This can save a lot of time.

The music industry is a big fan of the technology that is used by Ethereum. The music licensing company UJO is using this technology to receive payments and issue payments to their artists and the production staff. The money can be sent right to the people making the music. There is no need to involve the major labels which take a very high cut. This is something that is making the artists happy and they are able to get more of the money that they have worked for.

For those that want to invest in the latest technology Ethereum seems like a smart choice. Those who have taken the time to research this company are excited to invest in it and cannot wait to see where the company is going to go. On the Nasdaq Stockholm Exchange in Sweden investors are putting more and more money into this company. The Ether Tracker One and the Ether Tracker Euro have made $10 million in investments in the first week that they were open for trading.

Cryptocurrency is now considered to be a major asset by most people. They hold this currency to the same value that they would their cars, gemstones, real estate, as well as antiques. People are even looking to Ethereum for their retirement. The average investor is a person under the age of 45 years old. They are looking to invest in technology related companies.

In addition to sites such as Google and Amazon, Ethereum is another site that people are investing in for their future. Older investors are a little more cautious when it comes to these types of investments. They feel they do not have enough information about modern technology to make informed choices and are a little wary of these companies due to their newness in the market.

People are also looking to diversify their investments and not put all of their money into one place in case there is ever a problem. Today many people are looking to invest in crypto companies. They are growing large and have high earning potential. This is great for younger investors that are looking to diversify their portfolio while getting into profitable markets.

This site is very popular with people in their late 20s and 30s. This generation has grown up with technology and has seen how profitable it can be. They are also beginning to realize the importance of saving for retirement at an earlier age. They are looking for new and exciting investment accounts that will allow them to increase their profits. In addition to being able to increase their profits many younger investors like these also like that they can access their money if needed.

Sometimes life events happen such as marriage and paying for children to go to college. With Ethereum a person can have access to their money any time they want it. They do not have to leave it sit in an account for years. While with the ups and downs in the market it is recommended that a person wait it out for a couple of years, but there is the option to take out the money in case there is an emergency.

For many Ethereum is still a technology that is very new. Based on the results so far, this technology is impressive and can help a person make a lot of money on their investments. They can make money by buying and selling Ether. They can also add to their account by mining. The contracts will allow a person to keep more of their profit as well. Since there is no middle party that needs to get paid, this will allow more money to go into the pocket of the worker.

. The Future Of Ethereum

Ethereum is looking for ways to further improve their technology as well. They are looking to make this site easy for the average person to understand and use without any specialized technical knowledge. Cryptocurrencies are now becoming a major way that people are looking to invest. While there still are some concerns, there is a big increase in their market. Ethereum uses blockchains to increase security and takes additional measures to prevent hacking or unauthorized users for getting into the accounts.

They are looking to make things easy on all parties involved and are looking for a way for a person to increase their earnings from investments. Ethereum is setting the protocol for many other companies as well. They are sharing their technology so that everyone that is looking to invest online can be safe. There are a number of major companies that are adding to their security features and are taking lessons from Ethereum in how to prevent accounts from being subject to hackers.

Many businesses, especially those in the music industry, are looking to use this site in order to send payments. They cut out the third party. Not only does an artist get to keep more of their money, the transaction also travels through fewer hands. This will decrease the risk of a mistake being made or something happening during the transaction.

The price of Ethereum is one the rise as well. As people find out about this service there has been a huge increase on the percentage of the return. Each share of this company has increased and has gained more tokens. It is estimated that as long as the company continues to do well a person should see a nice return on their investment within a two-year period.

Ethereum is the way that the market is heading in the future. Many people are taking notice of this site and they are using it for their investments. People are using this site to buy and sell Ether. They are also using the online contracts to send and receive payments. Ethereum was once considered the way to invest in the future, but it is happening in the present. This site will allow a person to make a lot of money and they can do so from their home computer.

Conclusion

Thank you again for downloading this book!

I hope this book was able to help you .

Finally, if you enjoyed this book, then I'd like to ask you for a favor, would you be kind enough to leave a review for this book on Amazon? It'd be greatly appreciated!

Click here to leave a review for this book on Amazon!

Thanks!